Colors of GHANA

by Holly Littlefield
illustrations by Barbara Knutson

COLORS OF THE WORLD

Carolrhoda Books, Inc. / Minneapolis

I want to thank Shirley Hinson for all her help on this book and for introducing me to her beautiful country.—H.L.

The publisher wishes to thank Joseph Donkor for his help with the preparation of this book.

This book is available in two editions:
Library binding by Carolrhoda Books, Inc.
Soft cover by First Avenue Editions
Divisions of the Lerner Publishing Group
241 First Avenue North
Minneapolis, MN 55401 U.S.A.

Website address: www.lernerbooks.com

Library of Congress Cataloging-in-Publication Data

Littlefield, Holly, 1963–
    Colors of Ghana / by Holly Littlefield ; illustrations by Barbara Knutson.
      p.   cm. — (Colors of the world)
    Includes index.
    Summary: Explores the different colors found in Ghana's history, culture, and landscape.
      ISBN 1–57505–354–3 (lib. bdg.)
      ISBN 1–57505–374–8 (pbk.)
      1. Ghana—Juvenile literature. 2. Colors—Juvenile literature.
    [1. Ghana. 2. Color.] I. Knutson, Barbara, ill. II. Title. III. Series.
    DT510.L57 1999
    966.7—dc21   98-49496

Manufactured in the United States of America
    2 3 4 5 6 – SP – 04 03 02 01

Introduction

The country of Ghana offers a wide variety of landscapes, including tropical forests, a grassy savanna, and sandy beaches. It is located on the western coast of Africa. Bordering Ghana are Ivory Coast, Togo, Burkina Faso, and the Atlantic Ocean. Ghana is slightly smaller than the state of Oregon, but it contains an amazing variety of peoples, histories, cultures, and languages. Seventeen million people—belonging to nearly one hundred different ethnic groups—live in Ghana. Long ago, it was influenced by several empires, including the Ghana, the Mali, the Songhai, and the Asante. Since winning its independence from Britain, present-day Ghana has worked hard to bring schools, roads, electricity, and running water to all parts of the country. Although English is Ghana's official language, Ghanaians speak many other languages, such as Fante, Twi, Ewe, Ga, Nzema, Dagbani, and Hausa. The color translations in this book appear in Asante Twi.

3

Gold

Sika-futura (see-KAH FOO-too-roo)

A special **gold** stool is a symbol of Asante power and independence. It is called the Golden Stool. The Asante are one of the largest ethnic groups in Ghana. At one time, the Asante people belonged to a large empire divided into different areas. A king ruled each area. According to legend, this changed when the Golden Stool came to Earth from the sky. The people saw the stool as a sign to unite under one king. As a sign of respect, no person has ever been allowed to sit on the stool, not even the Asante king.

When the Asante were forced to join the British Empire, their new British governor demanded that the Asante turn the Golden Stool over to him. The Asante refused. Queen Nana Yaa Asantewaa led a battle to fight for the stool. The Asante lost the battle, but they hid the stool from the British for more than twenty years. Many thought that it had been lost. But after Ghana won its independence from the British, the stool was found. Some Asante believe that the soul of the nation lives in the stool. The Asante still carefully guard it.

White

Fi-taah (fee-TAH)

In some ethnic groups, both mother and baby wear **white** for the baby's naming ceremony, which takes place eight days after a child is born. Their white clothes represent a new beginning and new life. The baby's whole family—including grandparents, aunts, uncles, and cousins—are invited to the ceremony. A village elder formally presents the baby to the family. The elder announces the baby's name and tells the family what each part of the name means. Part of the name reveals if the baby is a girl or a boy and what day of the week the child was born. For example, if an Asante boy is born on a Friday, he is given "Kofi" as part of his name. If an Asante girl is born on a Friday, "Afua" will be part of her name. Children are also usually given another name in honor of a relative or close family friend and yet another name indicating whether they were born first, second, third, and so on. Sometimes Ghanaian children are also given an English name.

Orange

An-kaah (ahn-KAH)

Bright **orange** threads form the background of the vivid Kyeretwie kente cloth pattern. It is one of the many different Asante kente cloth patterns. Kente cloth is made from pieces of handwoven fabric. To make kente cloth, skilled craftspeople first weave intricate patterns in long strips of four-inch-wide fabric. Many of these strips are then sewn together to make a garment. It can take hundreds of hours to make just one piece of kente cloth. Each pattern has a different meaning. Some patterns stand for wealth, royalty, and elegance. Others stand for traits that Ghanaians value, such as courage, creativity, and loyalty. Some patterns are worn only by royalty or by important chiefs and their families.

The Kyeretwie pattern symbolizes bravery. It was designed to stand for warriors who proved their courage by catching a leopard. The black stripes running through this weaving represent the leopard's spots. Only the Asante chief could give permission to wear this pattern. Most Ghanaians still wear kente cloth for important ceremonies and other formal occasions. Many people consider it the national dress of Ghana. Although the Asante first created the cloth, other ethnic groups weave their own variations of kente cloth.

8

Gray

N-son (en-SON)

The **gray** walls of Elmina Castle stand as a grim reminder of the slave trade that took place in Africa for hundreds of years. When Europeans first came to the area that was later called Ghana, they built many fortresses and castles along the coast to help them control trade with the Africans. The Portuguese built the first of these fortresses in 1482. They called it Elmina, which means "the mine." In the beginning, Europeans came to Africa's western coast to find gold. But they found a way to make even more money—selling African people as slaves to other countries. Some African groups, such as the Asante, also participated in the slave trade. Some Asante sold slaves to the British. Millions of African people were chained and put in places like Elmina. Then these people were forced onto crowded ships, which carried them across the ocean to the Caribbean islands and the Americas. Many Africans died during this horrible journey across the ocean. Those who survived the trip faced a life of hard work on plantations and cruel treatment from slave owners. The slave trade came to an end in Ghana in the mid-1800s.

Green

Aha-ban (hah-BAHN)

Green plant life covers much of Ghana—with lush forests in the south and a grassy savanna in the north. Many Ghanaians believe that the land is meant to be shared with their ancestors and with those who have not yet been born. Therefore, they strive to respect the land and the wildlife and take care of them for future generations. The government has created many national parks and wildlife sanctuaries to protect the wide variety of plants and animals that live in Ghana. Elephants, buffalo, lions, leopards, and over three hundred different kinds of birds make their homes in the savanna, in Mole National Park. The Boabeng-Fiema Sanctuary protects several kinds of monkeys. They have become so used to humans that many monkeys are seen in the village of Boabeng as well as in the forest. Brightly colored butterflies, fruit bats, and antelopes also thrive in Ghana, and crocodiles sometimes lurk in the country's ponds and rivers.

Black

Tun-tum (toon-TOOM)

The **black** star in Ghana's flag represents Ghana's fight for freedom from European control. When Europeans first arrived, the Asante ruled much of south central Ghana. The Asante were skilled artists and craftspeople, especially famous for their work with gold. In fact, in the 1400s, the region became so well known for its gold that Europeans named the country the Gold Coast. After the Portuguese set up the first fortresses along the coast, the Dutch, the Danes, the British, and other Europeans all briefly ruled parts of Ghana. Then in 1901, after many bloody battles with the Asante, the British took control of the Gold Coast and made it a British colony. The Ghanaian people did not like living under British rule. They wanted to be in charge of their own country. In 1957, under the leadership of Kwame Nkrumah—from the Nzema ethnic group in western Ghana—they forced the British to leave. Then they changed the country's name from the Gold Coast to Ghana, after the ancient Ghanaian Empire of West Africa.

15

Tan

Ɔdote (doh-TEE)

Throughout Ghana, many drummers still use traditional Ghanaian drums, which are made by stretching **tan** animal skins across a wooden base. The base is often a section of a hollowed-out tree trunk. Ghanaian drums can be big—some are nearly five feet wide.

Drums are used at weddings, births, funerals, and other celebrations. Ghanaian drummers work hard to learn their craft. Young drummers usually become apprenticed to older ones, who will teach them the right tempos, patterns, and rhythms to use for each special event. One of Ghana's ethnic groups, the Ewe, even have a special ceremony to help link young drummers to the spirits of great drummers among their ancestors.

In many parts of Ghana, drummers are considered the keepers of the ethnic group's history and legends. Some Ghanaian drums, called talking drums, can imitate language with the different tones and tempos of their drums. Because of this, Ghanaian drummers can convey messages and tell stories without using words. Before phones and telegraphs became common in Ghana, drums were used to communicate messages across long distances.

17

Blue

Bu-ruu (BLOO)

The **blue** water of Lake Volta forms the largest artificially made lake in the world. It is more than three hundred miles long and covers more than three thousand square miles. It's about the size of Delaware and Rhode Island put together. This huge lake was made when the Akosombo Dam was built. More than seventy thousand people had to move from their homes to make way for the new lake. The dam controls the flow of the Volta River. The Akosombo Dam produces water for farming and generates all of Ghana's electricity.

Lake Volta is becoming an important place to raise fish. In addition, many people travel across Lake Volta by boat. The government is planning to add new ports in hopes of attracting even more boat travel.

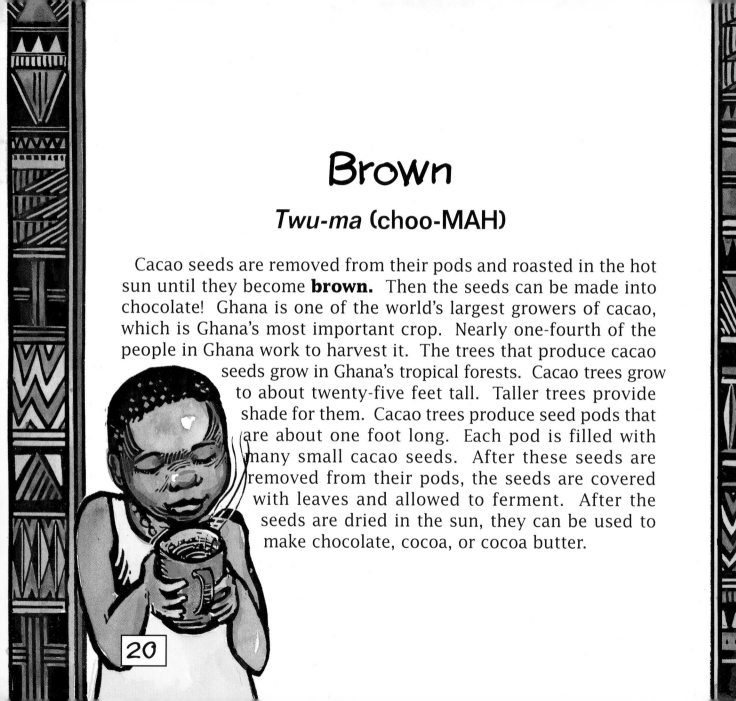

Brown

Twu-ma (choo-MAH)

Cacao seeds are removed from their pods and roasted in the hot sun until they become **brown.** Then the seeds can be made into chocolate! Ghana is one of the world's largest growers of cacao, which is Ghana's most important crop. Nearly one-fourth of the people in Ghana work to harvest it. The trees that produce cacao seeds grow in Ghana's tropical forests. Cacao trees grow to about twenty-five feet tall. Taller trees provide shade for them. Cacao trees produce seed pods that are about one foot long. Each pod is filled with many small cacao seeds. After these seeds are removed from their pods, the seeds are covered with leaves and allowed to ferment. After the seeds are dried in the sun, they can be used to make chocolate, cocoa, or cocoa butter.

20

21

Silver

Sri-ba (SREE-bah)

    According to Asante legend, a clever spider named Ananse hides in his **silver** web whenever he is in danger. Otherwise, this popular trickster lives and acts like a human. Ananse is greedy and lazy, but very clever. He also has a big appetite, and he never wants to share. In one story, Ananse and his family grow a great field of yams. But when it comes time to harvest the yams, Ananse decides that he does not want to share them with anyone, not even his wife and children. So he pretends to be dying and asks to be buried in his yam field. Then at night he sneaks out of his grave and eats and eats. When his family catches Ananse, they are surprised to see him alive. But tricky Ananse tells them that he has managed to return from the Kingdom of the Dead. Because he is such a good storyteller, Ananse's family and the people of the village believe him. Then the clever spider offers to tell the people about his experiences, but each person must pay a fee to hear the story.

23

Index